Ageing with Awareness

Ageing with Awareness

52 Contemplations for a Year of Weekly Inspiration

Felice Rhiannon

First printing: 2023

ISBN-13: 9798385601738

British Cataloguing Publication Data:

A catalogue record of this book is available from The British Library.

Also available for Kindle.

*The unripe cannot understand what it feels like
to be ready.*
Jalaluddin Rumi

*Not every old person is wise,
but you cannot become wise before you are old.*
Anonymous

To Caroline and Aleine
for their love, support and presence.

~

With deep gratitude to my maternal grandfather,
Iziel Krieger.

~

In joyful memory of Sandy Stone (1938-2023)
Fierce warrior,
Wise woman,
Inspired elder.

Foreword

Amidst the growing clamour of life, there lurks the constant, quiet possibility of moments of pause, drops of sweet water to a parched tongue. Our intoxication with external demands or internal turbulence, however, militates against the self-regard, sensitivity and poise required to stop for long enough to quench our deep thirst. Our daily preoccupations not only keep others' care (and their contention!) away from us, they keep us away from ourselves. And it is at that place of separation from ourselves and others that writing such as this comes into its own, urging, nudging us to reconnect.

Gifted to you by a true friend (who may be your wiser self), this book can (and will, if properly employed) help you put down your sword and shield and pause for long enough to touch into yourself and the flow beneath the surface of life.

The contemplations contained in this book urge us to slow down, stop and penetrate just beneath the skin of our everyday – as if, standing on a bridge, we direct our eyes for a moment away from our desired destination, downward to the flow of the water, and marvel at its ever-changing nature. If we do this for just long enough, we loosen the cords that tie us to the grindstone and catch a fresh glimpse of ourselves as unencumbered, liberated.

The experience of older age has every potential to be a charmed, perhaps the most charmed, phase of our life: our chance to immerse ourselves with awareness in both the tribulations and gifts of eldering. If we can respond with curiosity and openness, rather than reacting with pain and fear, we have the potential to be free to experience a life of greater service to other beings and the earth itself.

Felice Rhiannon's helpful distinction between 'older' and 'elder' is a challenge, stretching us out of any complacency or numbness we may feel about ageing into a space of wonder, where we may ask, "As I age, what of value is emerging in the lifelong event called 'me'?"

In all of us there is a voice capable of answering this question – not in a conclusive way, but in the way the rustling of leaves answers the wind. As the responses move through us, we start to reverse and redress the cruelty that has been done to ageing and older people by our linear, individualistic, achievement-obsessed culture, meeting instead with curiosity and respect for the emergent elder within us.

With the multi-faceted gems of our well-lived lives glinting in the debris of our wars upon self and others, calling us to greener, more peaceful places of interbeing, how can our world fail to profit from our awakening? This book points us in the direction of those pastures, reminding us that we are, in Felice's words, "the rapture of being alive".

Razia Aziz, December 2022
Speak-Scribe-Sing
www.waytu.co

Preface

This book, and I, owe deepest gratitude to Zalman Schachter-Shaolmi and my friend Susan Mashkes, who told me about his book *From Age-ing to Sage-ing*. In a fit of internalised ageism, I roundly rejected her mention of this book. A few years later, I had a dream about it and bought the book immediately. To say it changed my life sounds like a worn-out cliché. In this case, it is the truth.

Reb Zalman, as he is affectionately called, had a bit of a crisis in the year he was 60. What would his life be like from then on? How could he continue his intense travel and work schedule as he noticed changes in his energy and physical ability? Many of us have asked the same questions, with all their attendant emotions. He set out to explore the possibilities and created a pathway into what is now called 'conscious ageing' or 'elderhood'.

After the dream, and reading his book, I had a fire in my belly about conscious ageing. I mentioned this to a friend, and she said, "Why don't you write a blog about it?" My incredulous retort was: "Who would read it?" She then calmly replied, "It doesn't matter. Just put it out there."

So I did, and wrote more than 200 blog posts. Then the pandemic re-oriented my life. I no longer had the desire to write the blog. Instead, I wanted to go deeper, to contemplate what conscious ageing means, on all levels – physical, emotional, mental, political and spiritual. From the blog posts emerged these 52 invitations to you to do the same.

Much of the contents of this book evolved from my years at the OneSpirit Interfaith Seminary and the training to become a Certified Sage-ing Leader through Sage-ing International®, the organisation that grew from Reb Zalman's work. In those two transformative endeavours, I deepened into my self in ways I had not been able to before. They provided context for gentle, consistent inner exploration and growth. These 52 contemplations are the fruit of those inquiries.

Most importantly, I wanted to share with others the joy I experience in living as the ageing person I am. 'Meaning and purpose' have become buzz words, almost to the point of meaninglessness. However, conscious ageing has provided both for me as I live through my 70s and, hopefully, well beyond.

Please join me on this path to a rich, vibrant ageing, filled with companionship, joy, well-being and wisdom.

Introduction

The population in the United Kingdom, and other developed nations, is growing older. We are living longer, generally in better health and with greater opportunities than any older generation of the past.

Yet many of us feel undervalued, ignored and side-lined. We may feel our lives have lost purpose now we have left paid work. Or we may feel our role is limited to childcare – for the second time, with less energy this time around.

Others of us have found enormous freedom in these years. Suddenly, we find ourselves liberated to follow dreams of past decades that we were too busy to pursue at that time of life. Or an amazing new interest may have come our way unexpectedly.

Yet others of us have turned to service – mentoring younger people, volunteering in any one of a thousand ways, or taking action for the causes we support.

As we grow older, stepping onto a path that provides inspiration, challenge and excitement is the precious gift of conscious ageing. What exactly is conscious ageing?

The Conscious Aging Alliance notes: *"Conscious aging is a perspective that sees aging as a life stage full of potential for purpose, growth and service to community, and is a path toward realizing that potential."*

Within the covers of this book, you will discover 52

contemplations: explorations that support this potential. They provide a pause in which to reflect on the present, and your continued conscious development in this life stage.

Some will lead you into a quiet, internal space. Others might challenge your existing beliefs about ageing. Yet others are calls to action in the world. Any of them might strike a chord deep within you. I hope all of them will provide a week's worth of thought, feeling and adventure for your ageing process.

Over the course of a year, you will encounter weekly nourishment. You might read a contemplation once and allow it to percolate through the week. Or you might read the same one each day of the week before moving to the next. You might read them in order or choose one at random each week. Follow the rhythm your heart reveals throughout the year.

There is no right way to use this collection, just as there is no right way to grow older. We are unique beings with an individual flow and grace.

It is my deepest wish that these words bring joy, encouragement and energy to all your years.

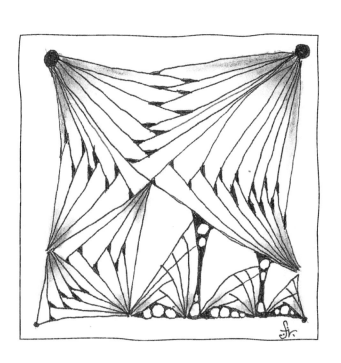

A Word about Words and Spelling

In compiling this small book, I faced a conundrum. I am an American living in England. Should I use British or American spelling? I decided, early on, to use British spelling, as this is the written language I now live. So, dear American readers, you will find the letter 'u' sprinkled in words you spell without them – honour/honor, for example – and 's' used where you might use 'z' – realise/realize, and 'e' where you don't expect it – ageing.

Another challenge I faced was the use of the word 'elder'. Some years ago, I began thinking of myself as an elder – someone who has grown from adulthood to elderhood. Using the words elderhood and elder indicate my respect for you as someone who has wisdom to share, creative energy to express, and an honoured place in the world.

At the same time, I am aware that the word has particular meaning and significance in several spiritual and religious traditions. Unless the word appears at the beginning of a sentence, it will not be capitalised. This will signify 'elder' as a life-stage, a developmental process we who live long enough have the privilege to grow into.

A Word About the Illustrations

The cover of this book, and the illustrations within it, are Zentangles®.

Zentangles are small pieces of unplanned black and white art, using a few repeated strokes in patterns. I think of them as meditations of heart, hand and pen, completely embracing the moment in a relaxed, enjoyable, mindful focus. There is no goal, no 'supposed to be'. A Zentangle is simply the bringing together of a few beautiful patterns in a small space. No previous training required!

A few years ago I became unable to hold a pen, or my wonderful knitting needles, for any length of time. A friend had mentioned Zentangles and I decided to 'train' my non-dominant hand – and the other side of my brain. Because this art form had no particular aim, it created the perfect field for experimenting, proving that no artistic skill is needed to 'tangle'.

The cover illustration is by Louise Gorst, my teacher. The interior tangles were drawn by me over a period of years and chosen to enhance your contemplations. Enjoy!

https://zentangle.com
https://tanglepatterns.com

i

I would know my shadow and my light.
So shall I at last be whole.
Then, courage brother, dare the grave passage.
Here is no final grieving,
But an abiding hope.
~~Anonymous

Light and shadow – that which we acknowledge and love about ourselves and that which we prefer not to see.

In the knowing, the deep will grieve. He does, however, tells us that the grieving is not final, not immutable. He asks that there be space: space for love.

The poet knew, perhaps for many years or possibly only for a short time, that both the light and the shadow are essential to our wholeness. On our precious planet it is the sun that creates shadow. We are grateful for the shadow of a parasol on a hot day. Nevertheless, we reject and ostracise our internal shadow.

These are the gritty bits of ourselves that generate the spark for the light. They are the places we rub up against in others and in ourselves. Often, the confrontation with shadow is painful. At the same time, it is the sunlight for our growth and evolution.

Elders often have the opportunity to look deeply into the shadow, and to heal the places that grate, that irritate, that hurt.

We have time and space to contemplate the ways in which the shadow might have wrought havoc in our lives.

We have time and space to make amends, where appropriate and possible, and to re-frame those experiences.

We have time and space to grieve.

We have time and space to be our wholeness.

We have time and space to dare to find abiding hope.

We have time and space to dare to find love.

ii

Arriving is a continual process... a process of acceptance.
~~Charlotte Watts [i]

These simple words echo what we can learn from our ageing process. We are constantly arriving into each moment, each breath, each aspect of who we are, each step of unfolding.

Each arrival can be a lesson in acceptance as we become more deeply aware of what ageing, and eldering, means.

Our physical selves change almost daily... skin, hair, waistline, muscles, joints, digestion. Our mental selves also experience continual shifting... the capacity to respond to new information, memory, the ability to concentrate and focus, organisational skill. Finding acceptance of these changes is often challenging, difficult and even painful. Other times, the acceptance flows with grace and ease.

Our emotional selves also experience change with the passing of years. We have had many moments of deep love, grief – with their accompanying tears – irritation (and sometimes incandescent anger), unimaginable joy, bubbles of laughter arising from the silliest events. Each of these shifts in our emotional landscape asks us to inquire and accept them as they flow like a river in the heart.

Alongside all these changes, something remains steady, true, unerring. The connection to Spirit, and the deepening of that connection, grows with each passing day. Sometimes this growth is imperceptible, known only in retrospect. Other times, there is a growth spurt, much like our physical selves experienced many decades ago. An insight or an enlightening perception arises, seemingly from nowhere.

We never know what these changes might be, or when and how they might arrive. We can commit to stay awake to their arrival.

Arrival into and acceptance of each one is essential to the world.

This is part of the mystery of elderhood.

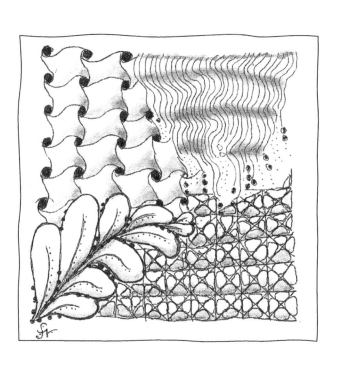

iii

In Japan there is a tradition of Zen Buddhist monks and nuns writing death poems. The poems can be written at any time of life or at the author's imminent death. Almost universally, they contain a meaningful observation on life. This verse was written by the renowned poet of the Edo period (15th century), Matsuo Basho.

Autumn night
Don't think your life
Didn't matter.

It is an autumn night, a life approaching near to its end. It is a time of reflection, of introspection, of contemplation.

At this moment we might reflect on the challenges, losses and accomplishments of a lifetime. We may acknowledge the good we have done, the love we have shared. There may be thoughts of 'Not good enough', 'Not enough', 'I'll just sit and wait to die'.

We might take these reflective moments to know deeply inside that all life matters. We are all important energies in the world, regardless of what we have done or not done. We are each unique, a facet on the jewel of life.

In the autumn of life, we have the capacity to reframe and repair, to find forgiveness in ourselves, both for ourselves and others. We might find ourselves transforming the paradigm of ageing. It is in the autumn of life that we have enough experience to grow wisdom, and to manifest that wisdom as a gift to all those whose lives we touch.

No matter what the season outside the window, the autumn of life is filled with boundless potential when we live it with curiosity, compassion and open-heartedness. Each day can be filled with adventure, even when we can't leave the chair in the sitting room. It might be inner adventures that fill our life in its autumn.

It might be then, in the autumn, that we know that our life matters.

iv

With so many people living longer, there has been a lot of interest in ancestry. People are finding relatives they didn't know they had, sometimes with great joy and other times with regret and sorrow. The search into the past brings it into the present and affects the future. The search for ancestors, the connection with those who preceded us, can allow for life repair and forgiveness, as well as deep learning.

Where we are right now, who we are right now, sets the stage for our future. We are the ancestor of our future selves. David Whyte, in his poem Coleman's Bed, invites us to "Live in this place as you were meant to and then, surprised by your abilities, become the ancestor of it all..."

First, we "live in this place", as we are meant to.

Be present.

Become conscious of all that we experience.

Breathe into each moment, as we are meant to.

Find our seat at whichever table we discover ourselves.

Be willing to live fully, as we are meant to.

Take risks, for we may have less to lose than we had when we were younger.

Perhaps now our ego is a bit less invested in what others

might think of us. Perhaps now we are more willing to be fully who we were meant to be.

Then we will be "surprised by our abilities". Our decades of life experience is what we bring to that table. Whatever wisdom we have gained speaks to the others at the table. By claiming our seat, we live in that place fully embodied, fully realised, as we are meant to. And no one will be more surprised than ourselves at what we know and share now, and what wisdom is, as yet, unspoken.

In taking our place fully, we become the ancestor of our own future. With each action, with each word, with each breath we create our present. At the same time, we write our legacy. The legacy we leave is the one we live now.

We then are truly worthy ancestors, as we are meant to be.

υ

On a crisp autumn day, I walked along the familiar pavement near my home. I saw approaching me a toddler with her mum. She was holding a large, bright fallen leaf, twirling it so its jewel colours glinted in the sunshine. Several people stopped to comment on the leaf's beauty and how adorably cute the little girl was.

Needless to say, she was a bit unsteady on her feet and walked at a very slow pace, supported by her mum and the handle of the buggy. She needed help to navigate the uneven paving, the tree roots and the oncoming pedestrians.

A few months later, as I walked along on a crisp winter day, an older woman walked along the same street. She was a bit unsteady on her feet and walked at a very slow pace, mindful of the uneven pavement and the passers-by. She too was supported. Her hands rested on the handles of a Zimmer frame/walker and her carer was right next to her.

No one stopped to comment on her courage or her strength.

No one stopped to admire her white hair.

No one stopped to chat with her or her carer.

No one stopped.

In fact, other pedestrians simply whizzed past her with

disgruntled looks on their faces, wishing this old lady would get out of their way as they hurried to the important coffee date in the cafe on the corner.

Same pace.

Same support.

Very different responses.

vi

Giving birth is seen as the domain of the young, those with energy and vigour, those who can bear the burden of new life.

Elders too can give birth. We, with decades of experience, can also bear the burden of the new. Creative energy thrives in the fecund ground of our ageing. In fact, we have been giving birth for decades in the work we have done, the poetry we have written, the relationships we have formed, the laughter and tears we have shared.

All that we have lived has arisen from the unborn, from the spark of our lifeforce. We may have had the assistance of a midwife or two in the form of teachers, mentors, friends and lovers who helped us transform the unknown into the manifest.

We elders, over the decades, have created and witnessed the emergence of the new – from technological innovation to artistic endeavours, from the unexpected to the now commonplace. We have catalysed all of it from vibrant inner desire.

Universal creativity continues to flow in each of us. There may now be limitations, which, instead of hindering us, might become the source of innovation and far-reaching vision. While the physical capacity of our resourceful selves may vary, the energy to give birth remains. We have had sufficient experience to accept uncertainty in our creative process, and to allow space and time for the unknown to arise into the known.

This adventurous spirit might unfold as a meaningful conversation with a friend, or a new computer app, or a walk in the woods, mindfully noting all that lives there, or a sophisticated analysis of a challenging book. This artful liveliness might transform into a profound contemplation, breathing into the present moment. A mature elder might enjoy a playful time with a younger, dancing to the latest pop music.

Elders hold wonder and delight alongside the gravitas of our years. Deepening awareness opens doors to creative energy that might have been closed in decades past. Now, in this life stage, we have a different vigour, a renewed energy of creation. We can birth the gifts of new ventures, new life.

vii

Having lived into our elderhood, we might at times wonder about the possibility of dying tomorrow or living another decade or two. Should we regard each day as a bonus and live for the now, or make long-term plans for an unknown future?

Both/and!

One aspect of our well-earned elder wisdom is the ability to let go of either/or thinking and embrace both/and.

Each day is a gift, if you like. It offers another opportunity to smile, to dance, to breathe, to love.

At the same time, planning for the long term is a wise endeavour. It answers a basic human need for some semblance of security. Taking care of adequate shelter for the coming years, along with some form of health care, a will, an advance directive and powers of attorney all make perfect sense as part of an elder's life. They allow us to relax into our elderhood freer from some anxieties.

This advance planning may present challenges in our relationships with siblings, partners or children. These conversations allow us to open what are often thorny enquiries. Importantly, they give us space to make our wishes known, possibly regarding our funeral.

With the material plane sorted out we can take time to reflect on our inner tasks. We might choose to write or record an 'ethical will', or a life history, or a letter to someone loved dearly. The task of forgiveness often becomes apparent during this inner inquiry; forgiveness to be offered or accepted. This intimate review could perhaps bring to awareness both the lessons easily learned over a lifetime and those we garnered from our severe teachers.

Living each day as a gift and long-term planning are not mutually exclusive. In fact, the planning can make living fully more possible. The living of each day, being as present as possible, might make the planning easier and more authentic. We can do BOTH!

viii

Sitting, as we've done thousands of times, there is suddenly a sensation in the hip or knee or back. Maybe it joins the party of other similar sensations. Are they pains? Aches? Niggles?

Our problem-solving brain switches into high gear. What to do about it? Acupuncture? Osteopathy? Painkillers? Hip replacement?

Breathe.

One breath at a time.

Letting go of fear.

Releasing the agitated mind.

Discovering again the unchanging, ever-present ground of being.

Love.

Connection.

Breathe.

What does it mean for a body to age, change, transform from what it was to what it is in each moment? Our body has never been the same, from day to day, from year to year. It has always been ageing, since the moment we were conceived. It has hurt and ached before. And yet, somehow, this is different. This body is now old, less able, less agile, more vulnerable.

Breathe.

We, as elders, can allow our heart also to be more vulnerable. We can open more fully to our connection with all that is, including our physical self. The sensitive heart is also on the path of growing older, of ageing. We become more able and more agile in this, perhaps an undiscovered or less familiar aspect of ourselves.

Breathe.

A different facet of the jewel we are now can shine more brightly. As we learn to breathe into it, the heart space glows as we continue to grow deeper. It allows us to illuminate the world around us, those closest to us and those more distant. It enlightens the physical, material plane, shining into our discomfort.

Breathe.

This brilliance can be perceived in each breath. The light of this jewel can be polished again each time we choose to stop, to look, to sense, to open to its glory – each time we are vulnerable to its dignity – each time we breathe like a bellows to clear the mind and heart. We can share this light as we grow, as we grow older.

Breathe into our ageing body.

Breathe into our expanding heart.

ix

Many of us, in our elderhood or earlier, have attended yoga classes. In every one of them you hear a sigh of gratitude when the teacher says, "Please prepare yourself, and get what you need, for our final relaxation." Those two words, 'final relaxation', are a recent interpretation of the Sanskrit *shavasana* – the pose of the corpse. The word 'relaxation' is much more palatable and inviting, much less frightening. Can we truly relax into 'corpse-hood' after a yoga class? At any time?

This pose is actually yoga's – and life's – greatest challenge. In the 5 or 10 minutes of class time allotted for this pose we are transformed into a corpse, in the same way as we embodied a triangle or a warrior in the active yoga practice. Within the stillness of the body, we are asked to maintain complete awareness as we engage with *shavasana*. At the same time, there is a letting go, releasing to the support of the floor and the warmth of the blanket, often lulling us to sleep.

Can we conceive of ourselves as dead? Probably not. However, we can practise reflecting that our life, as we have known it until this moment, is over.

Each moment is a death, a passing of time, never to be reclaimed. Each breath is unique and will never be repeated. Each heartbeat, a manifestation of consciousness beyond words, can only happen once in a lifetime. Each thought passes through our mind-field in its singular form, never to be repeated in exactly the same way. Each blink bathes the eyes in that moment only.

Knowing this, we can commit to taking what is left to us before becoming a corpse – the next moment, the following breath, the succeeding heartbeat – and live it with curiosity, purpose and passion.

We can, as we lie still on the yoga mat (actual or metaphoric), breathing consciously, live in a vast, unbounded space of this moment.

We can, in the tranquillity of *shavasana*, be free.

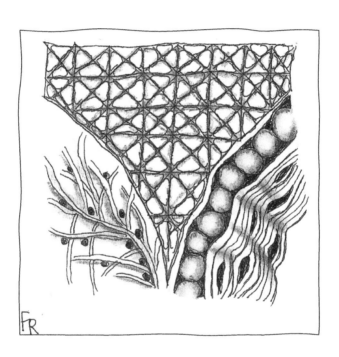

x

Often, it is ceremony or ritual that allow us to fully experience life's joys and sorrows. We share these experiences with the vast majority of humans. We have more in common than we have differences, and ceremonies allow us to share these universal states of being. Most cultures have ways to celebrate and ways to grieve, ways to mark the passage of time.

There are daily rituals: bathing, dressing, preparing and eating meals, meditating and praying (in whatever form appeals).

There are occasional rituals: marking a day of rest, celebrating a union, marking a life passage, celebrating the seasonal turning of the year.

And there are once-in-a-lifetime ceremonies: birth and death.

In these ceremonies and rituals, we find the cadence of life. Just as in the rhythm of day and night, exhale and inhale, these events mark personal and collective time. They unite us in mysterious ways as well as material ways. They support us in times of sorrow and times of rejoicing.

In many cultures there are ceremonies for youngers, though not many for elders. We can, however, create ceremonies as ways to honour our elderhood. Stepping across the threshold from adulthood to elderhood is as vital a step in our development as the one from childhood to adolescence, or adolescence to adulthood. Such a ceremony can allow us to take on the mantle of the elder, the wise one.

In your creative imagination, form a living picture of a ceremony that marks your acceptance of elderhood. Imagine it vividly. How old are you? How do you prepare for the ceremony? What do you wear? Who is invited? (And who is not welcome?) Where does it take place? In a grassy field or a formal hall or in a sacred space? How is the space decorated? Is there music or silence? Dance? Do you imagine a feast? What do you eat and drink?

Who holds the space for your passage into elderhood, and supports the guests in their witnessing? What words are spoken? Who participates in the ceremony itself? Friends? Lovers? Children? Is there a lasting symbol of this ceremony, so you can remember it in years to come? How does the ceremony end?

How do you become, and then be, an elder?

xi

In Buddhist thought we meet the concept of the 'near enemy'. We can think of near enemies when we look at a world map, noting how often borders shift and governments change, sometimes creating very near enemies.

This Buddhist concept though has more to do with our inner geography than any outer frontier. We embody the near enemy when we mistake one emotional state for something very similar. We might believe we are expressing compassion when, in truth, we are experiencing pity. Or we might justify our unenviable indifference as the desirable traits of equanimity and calm.

These are subtle shades of emotional experience that ask us to be mindful and truthful with ourselves. In this inquiry we might find that the 'near enemy' is as close as our own skin.

As we age, we acquire wrinkles, weight, grey hair, brown spots. Can we be truthful about these borders between one life stage and another? How close are our outer near enemies? How near are our inner near enemies?

We buy creams, pills, potions, supplements and prescription drugs, all in the name of staying young. How near is the enemy of inner denial to the outer appearance of youth? Is this image the near enemy of our reality?

With the mind-heart of the elder, we can enquire deeply.

The truth lies in the relationship of the two aspects of the near enemy. In contemplating and sitting with our outer image, we offer ourselves the opportunity to embrace the reality of each wrinkle and the wisdom it enfolds. We might find in our flesh a relaxation and comfort in the surrender to gravity. As each grey hair emerges, the truth of the transition of ageing becomes clear for all to see.

It is in the willingness to see and then acknowledge this truth that the elder can become an influencer. We can model and enjoy our shifts from one form to the next, from one stage of life into the evolution of the next. By rejecting the idea of fake news about ourselves, we find the freedom that lives in truth. With this awareness we, the elders, display our value to society and make our presence a felt sense in those we encounter. We move from the confusion of the near enemy to the clarity of our deepest selves.

xii

Come, come, whoever you are. Wanderer, worshiper, lover of leaving. It doesn't matter. Ours is not a caravan of despair. Come, even if you have broken your vows a thousand times. Come, yet again, come, come.
~~ Jelaluddin Rumi

These words often inspire those on a spiritual path to return after departing the "caravan", often in "despair". We might find ourselves, after making a commitment to pray or meditate or practise chi gong or yoga, becoming less enthusiastic, less determined to practise. The habit diminishes, then fades altogether. A while later we become aware that something is missing, something that nourishes us is absent, that it is we who have been diminished.

Our human nature can lead us to create other priorities as life unfolds. Suddenly, other things seem more important. The calendar becomes too full and something needs to be deleted. Often it is the time we have set aside for connection, for introspection, for quiet contemplation. The busy-ness of outer demands can encroach on our inner world.

Yoga tradition suggests a few ways to counter the human foible of moving "away from that which is beneficial to us and toward that which is harmful". Connecting with a spiritual companion might open the door again. Reading inspiring words can bring us back to the "caravan". A community of support where we share, with like-minded people, our successes and our challenges helps to keep us focused.

No matter how we re-dedicate ourselves, we can return. There is no punishment or banishment. There is no condemnation, even after a thousand leavings.

It is heart-warming to know we can return. We can join Rumi in his caravan. We can "come, come" to re-unite with our companions and connect again with whatever calls us, by whatever name or namelessness, whether in form or formlessness.

In the many decades we have lived, there have been many leavings and many returnings. This process contributes to the rich wisdom we hold. As we experience our elderhood, we know, deep down, the leaving and returning is the rhythm of our path, our life.

Thank you, Rumi.

xiii

Compassion is one of the foundations of the world's spiritual traditions. It is an inner response to suffering and then acting on that response. These traditions illuminate compassion as neither passive nor sentimental. Instead, they ask us to act.

At its core, compassion instils in us the realisation that we are interdependent. The Buddha, two thousand years ago, continuously taught this principle, which has been supported by contemporary science. Meister Eckhart, a 14th century German Catholic theologian, mystic and philosopher, also teaches us about compassion when he said, "Whatever happens to another, be it a joy or sorrow, happens to me." The word itself means 'to suffer together'; to live together, knowing that we have all suffered.

Our elder lifespan has seen us through countless joys and sorrows. Thus, we have become what Elisabeth Kubler-Ross, the 20th century pioneer in the exploration of grief, called "beautiful people".

Beautiful people, all of us in our elderhood, have known defeat and success, gain and loss, struggle and ease, joy and suffering. We have grown an appreciation, a sensitivity, an understanding of life. We have found a way into these deep experiences that can guide us into a life of loving concern, a life of compassion, a life of active caring.

We, the beautiful people, haven't just happened. Our long

lives have, gently or harshly, filed away the rough edges of the ego so we can respond to the suffering of others with compassion. This response of the heart may find us involved in actions for social justice or adding prayer to our spiritual practice. We may be moved to write a spiritual legacy for those younger than we are, expressing our concern for them and for the world.

We might respond to our inner call of compassion by reaching out to a friend who is ill or lonely. We may adopt a rescue animal or volunteer at a shelter for women or refugees. Or we may naturally open our hearts to the suffering of all beings. These actions, small and large, are inherent to our human nature.

In this stage in our lives, we have the opportunity not only to act from compassion, but to model it for others. We might think of compassion as a hallmark of elderhood, an emblem of a beautiful person.

xiv

The root of the word courage is *cor* – the Latin word for heart. Courage originally meant 'to speak one's mind by telling all one's heart'. Over time, this definition has changed. Today, courage is more synonymous with being heroic.

The courageous elder is both – an heroic person who speaks from the heart. It takes courage to be a compassionate, visible older person in a society that generally holds its elders with disdain bordering on contempt, certainly with little or no respect.

Speaking the truth of our experience asks us to be bold. It demands a big heart, a heart that will step into a place of fear and then act from the deepest place of inner peace. Whether we step into a protest march for what we believe or speak our truth to those we love, a big heart is often called upon to act.

Like other aspects of who we are, courage takes practice. This practice asks us to find our voice, a voice full of compassion and caring. At the same time, courage expresses its strength and commitment, learned over decades of life experience. Sometimes, it might demand that we find a safe space to rage before our elder-courage can become a visible reality.

We can also grow our courage in quiet ways, finding the voice of calm in the solitude of our meditative/contemplative practice, whether it be prayer, centring, journaling, walking or formal sitting practice.

We can find our heroic, truthful, elder self with others. Sharing together, knowing you are not alone in speaking your truth, makes space for your courage to emerge. Joining other courageous, like-hearted people increases the joy and aliveness of taking action, whatever that might be.

Courage is the most important of all virtues, because without it we can't practice any other virtue with consistency.
~~ Maya Angelou (American poet, author 1928-2014)

xv

In our 20s and 30s, we had a lot of 'fluid intelligence'. This type of smarts increased through those earlier decades and enabled us to work hard, solve problems and analyse situations with focused attention. As we worked harder with this form of our intelligence, it increased faster, making us inventive and skilled at our chosen occupation. This type of intelligence, psychologists tell us, makes us good at what we do. It also decreases as we age.

We elders, whose fluid intelligence wanes, can be seen as irrelevant and without value when our attention moves away from working harder. Not surprisingly, we have an unacknowledged and under-valued form of intelligence that increases in our 40s and 50s and beyond, called crystallised intelligence. We might prefer to call it *crystalline* intelligence.

This remarkable power allows wisdom to grow along with the ability to pass that wisdom and acquired knowledge to others. We know a lot, and we know what to do with what we know. It functions alongside the skills we have acquired, adding decades of accomplishment to creating new pathways for creativity that are different from focus and hard work.

It is now our task to move consciously from the younger form of intelligence to inhabit and celebrate our present wisdom. We move into the arena of teacher, mentor, guide. Though somewhat mysterious, such a quality doesn't prevent us from learning new things, working with focus, or bringing our analytical abilities to bear on a problem.

This crystalline intelligence is in good company. The oldest known pieces of our planet's surface are 4.4-billion-year-old zircon crystals from the Jack Hills of western Australia[ii]. Our elder wisdom, crystalline in nature, puts us in harmony with the planet!

Embracing this newer/older intelligence places elders in a role long honoured by Indigenous peoples. The elder holds the stories of the tribe and passes those stories from lived experience to the youngers. We too pass on our decades of living, in whatever community we find ourselves, simply by being authentically crystalline.

xvi

All that we will take across the waters of death is the jewel of love.
~~Jalāl al-Dīn Rumi

As we have grown older, we have acquired the wisdom to appreciate love's vital role in life, to express that love and to cultivate it. Love, as a treasure, grows in bedrock, formed by pressures and shifts in our deepest mines. To extract love, we delve into unseen caverns, with conscious attention and an open heart. To inspire ourselves with the crystalline gem of love is one of the reasons for our being on the planet, bringing the glory of the core to the surface.

Our continued opening to love gives us courage to live honestly and passionately, even in the face of love's pain and disappointment and grief. In some ways, love itself is a kind of death. Love empowers us to open and let go of the long-held, hardened parts of ourselves, the metallic armour that has kept love away.

Love supports us in being with what is, in delight as well as sorrow and desolation. Love holds us, like a timber in a mine, when we surrender our need to have the world be exactly as we would want it. We can thus step into the radiance of truth and release our expectations and inauthenticity in favour of love.

Each of these deaths contributes to the softening of the ego that many spiritual traditions encourage. With a less defended ego, we elders can take our shining place in the world with courage and curiosity, strength and resilience. Elders willing to die these small deaths find themselves in the luminous world of love and truth.

These deaths are our guides into the splendour of love, the diamond of the open heart and the pearl of wisdom.

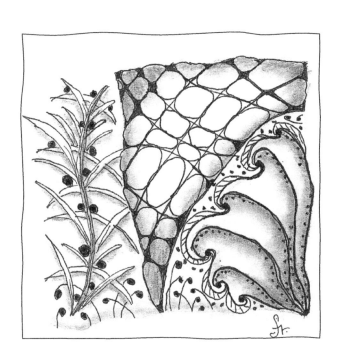

xvii

Do you remember the polio vaccine? At first, it was an injection invented by Dr Jonas Salk. Some years later, it was administered orally on a sugar cube. This advance that tasted good and didn't hurt was formulated by Albert Sabin. Though neither Salk (1914–1995) nor Sabin (1906–1993) received a Nobel Prize for their efforts, most baby boomers remember the fear of a polio epidemic and the solutions these men created.

Rarely, though, do we think of either of them as elders until we remember that Salk said, "Our greatest responsibility is to be good ancestors." While his creation saved countless thousands of lives during his lifetime, his focus was on the future, on generations yet to come. He left a legacy that literally changed the health of the world.

While each of us may not change the world as a whole, our legacy will change a small part of it. What is legacy? We usually think of it as material – which person will inherit which asset.

We can also leave an ethical legacy, a spiritual one based on our values. This can take the form of a written document. It might be a letter written to the people who are important to you. It might be attached to your will. It might take the form of a voice or video recording.

Your legacy might be as immediate as what you say in a meeting, around the dining table or at a party. It might be a book you've written, or a painting or a poem you've created. It might be the work you have done in your decades-long career.

Or it might simply be your presence, your authenticity, your willingness to grow into your elderhood. This may be the most important legacy you can leave. There will be a trace of that energy that graces each person you meet. You will have touched something deep in them that ripples out to all their connections.

While I imagine Salk and Sabin had an idea of how their legacy would affect the world, they can't possibly have known that polio is now all but eradicated across the globe.

We too have no idea how our legacy might influence the future. In spite of not knowing, its creation is worth our best effort.

xviii

What can we do today, in the present, that our future self, the one that is born in the next present moment, will thank us for?

It certainly wouldn't be the long to-do list shortened by the accomplishment of a few tasks.

Yoga practice?

Reading the long-postponed novel, just for fun?

A walk in the sunshine?

Self-forgiveness?

A phone call, not an email, to a friend?

A smile?

Today, we might find a very simple answer – a quiet cup of tea, a simple sitting while looking out the window at the sky just as it is. The tea is important to our future self because of the moment-to-moment experience of heat, liquid, spicy flavour, the enjoyment of the senses. And the looking is important to our future self for no particular reason! The space created inside, in silence, is a reflection of, and reflected by, the sky.

It is the space of potential that is vitally important for our future self. It is the only importance. The filling of the space, or not filling of the space, may, or may not, be important.

In this moment, only the potential, along with the tea, are essential to our future self.

xix

Ram Dass, one of the 20th and 21st centuries' great spiritual teachers, reminds us to grieve. We usually think of grieving as a process after the death of someone close. He reminds us there are other losses to be honoured.

We must take enough time to remember our losses – be they friends or loved ones passed away, the death of long-held hopes or dreams, the loss of homes, careers, or countries, or health we may never get back again. Rather than close ourselves to grief, it helps to realize that we only grieve for what we love.

In our long lives we have experienced many losses. Have we truly grieved them? Have we truly surrendered to the fact of life that is a death? Have we truly acknowledged the love that makes each of those grievings possible?

Looking back on scores of years, thousands of days, we have the opportunity to grieve. We can slow down enough to recall the significant events and people in our life, honouring their role and grieving their end. We can explore memories – painful, challenging, joyful – and grieve their passing. We might also take the opportunity to repair any harm done, if possible. We can open to the process of forgiveness, for ourselves and others, that often accompanies grief.

In our grieving, we permit a spacious centre where more life can unfold. This space is often ignored, skipped over.

We are told to "get on with it" when a dear one dies. When a dream is lost to the ravages of time or circumstance, we are told to "move on". When we lose anything we cherish – an heirloom, a home, a field recently covered with asphalt – taking the time to grieve allows for the completion of the cycle of its life. We can then, without forgetting, rejoice in whatever might arise in the space they occupied.

Now freedom is more available, the breath flows more easily and, when the time comes to step into our own dying, there will be no ungrieved loss holding us back.

Now we are more available to love.

xx

If I am not for myself, who will be for me?
If I am not for others, what am I?
And if not now, when?

This often misquoted and misattributed Jewish aphorism was written by Hillel the Elder, a leader of the Jewish people, who lived in Babylon and Jerusalem, purportedly from 110 BCE to 10 CE.

His title 'the Elder' is a light shining in the doorway to our own elderhood. We can learn many lessons about spiritual eldering from these three short sentences.

We must be for ourselves, care for ourselves, love ourselves, trust and honour ourselves. Without this energy, no one can be for us. Without a sense of our value, no one else will value us. We must speak and live our truth or lose all sense of integrity and wholeness. For many of us, our elder years give us just this opportunity.

It is as a whole person that we can surrender the ego self to be for others. We can aspire to release the obstacles that armour our heart so we can be of service. We can listen with compassion and care. Hillel asks: "What am I?" not "Who am I?" What are we if we cannot be available, willing to be challenged when we encounter difference, and open to dialogue? We would be frightened, demagogic, narcissistic, unfeeling and shut down to the possibilities of authentic heart-space relationships.

Lastly, "If not now, when?" We have only the now. Action can only take place in the now. With the strength of spiritual connection as our foundation, we can act to change how we live with ageing, dying and death. While we may not live as long as Hillel the Elder supposedly did, we can aspire to die as our fullest selves, elders who contributed to a shift in consciousness.

We might also aspire to live and die honouring the other of Hillel's most well-known teachings: "That which is hateful to you, do not do to your fellow. That is the whole Torah[iii]; the rest is explanation; go and learn."

Thank you, Hillel, for what you have given the world... and to eldering.

xxi

Looking into a still pond, seeing the reflection of sky and trees and possibly our own face, we are given a gift of beauty, of clarity. Reflecting on our life gives us the opportunity to see more vividly our decades of experience. This becomes the spiritual task of life review or, better said, life-reviewing, for this is a continuous, active path to the wisdom of the elder.

Reflecting is different from reminiscing. When we reminisce, we simply remember the past, usually the romanticised 'good stuff'. In reflecting, we have the ongoing opportunity to change course, to modify our behaviour, to learn. As we take on the task of life-reviewing, we can find opportunities to mend our ways and possibly make amends to those we might have hurt.

Re-viewing, with compassion and tenderness for the uncomfortable, opens the door in our heart to self-forgiveness.

We also reflect on our achievements, our successes, our ongoing aliveness. This is an area of life we are taught to minimise, lest we seem arrogant. Yet, in acknowledging our accomplishments, we step into a profound truth. We can re-cognise (to know again) our triumphs in the light of the honest reflection we see in the still water of the pond. We can see a complete picture of a life.

In this process, we take responsibility for today and for

yesterday, opening a present and a future that is more authentic, more loving. While we may not be able to repair all those years of interactions, we are not powerless in creating more authentic and lively relationships in the now – with ourselves and with others, with our community and the planet.

Life-reviewing can be an exciting, intimate adventure. It reveals the trajectory of a life examined, with all its bumps and potholes, with all its glowing sunrises and starry skies, with all its awe-ful beauty.

xxii

It is permitted.

You may do this.

You may begin the story of your life right now, in this present moment.

It is permitted.

Each moment provides us the opportunity to re-frame disempowering thoughts and images we might carry from our distant past. We can, with a compassionate, tender and open heart, forgive ourselves and others. Each one of us has experienced hardship and pain. Those experiences have left scars. We can provide the soothing balm to heal those hurts and minimise the scars.

It is permitted.

Yes, it takes courage and determination. We find the willingness to look, to understand and then to see the gift in each of those hurts. We would not be the people, the elders, we are today without them. Some of the gifts may be hard to discover, hard to understand. Allowing an open space for growth allows the gift to become clear.

It is permitted.

This healing may bring tears of re-lived pain, or tears of relief, or tears of joy. We are now able to experience deep acceptance of our past and deep gratitude for the wisdom we have gained through it.

It is permitted.

Life now begins with a new perception, a different understanding of what has pained us. A lightness might grow inside, a load relieved, a wound healed. Now begins the life of a more liberated elder, a life unfolding in freedom. No external source has told us. We know from within.

It is permitted.

What difference do we now experience daily, in each breath, in each moment, living inside that freedom? What growth and change opens in our relationships? What sense of ourselves evolves?

Let us write the story of our new life now.

It is permitted.

xxiii

Who am I?

Who have I been?

Who might I be in 5, 10, 15 years?

Western astrologers tell us that approximately every 28 years Saturn returns to the position in the sky it was in when we were born. This can be a time of reflection, upheaval and change.

28. 56. 84.

At 28, most of us reflect, with more or less angst, about our place in the world, our identity in the larger scheme of things. As elders, we might reflect back. What decisions did we make then? How did those decisions shape the rest of our lives?

The opportunity (astrologically speaking) arises again at 56. We are now closer to 60 than 50. This might have been a frightening thought! Like the Buddha, we might have begun to think of old age, illness and death. While we hoped to have more years to live fully, in the deepest part of ourselves we knew the inevitable was creeping closer.

At some point in our cycle of musings we might realise that it made no difference that we were successful or unsuccessful at something, or that we were or were not a partner or parent. It made no difference if we owned or didn't own a car or a house. It made no difference if we had or didn't have a title or a dream job. Nor did it make a difference if we were a woman or a man, straight or gay or bi or trans, blonde or brunette, bald or full-headed, dyed or natural. All those identities ceased to matter.

Our identities change many times in a lifetime. Elders, who have lived long, have the opportunity to discover that what truly matters is that which is unchanging.

And what is that? What is it that doesn't change? What is the essence?

As we age, we often remark that we don't 'feel' 60 or 70 or 80. What we might actually feel is our continuing life force and we identify that force with the time we were in our teens or 20s, our younger time. This is the same life force that now, in this present moment, enlivens our eldering time.

Today, now, do we identify as an 'old' person? Do we aspire to let go of all identities? Can we elders be spontaneous, a trait usually associated with the young, now? Can we open to the present moment without the filters of age, gender, culture, conditioning?

Can we identify with the eternal?

Can we be aware of awareness itself?

This is an aspiration.

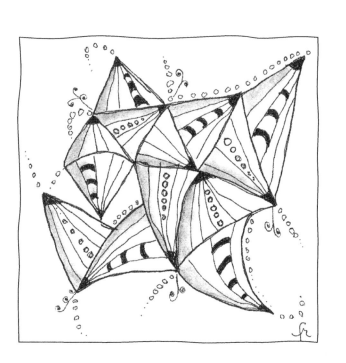

xxiv

Forty or so meditators gathered in a London university lecture hall. They listened as monks and nuns from the lineage of the revered master

Thic Nhat Hanh spoke, imparting their teacher's lessons, echoing his wisdom. The meditators sat in silence, each taking what they could into their heartmind.

Then came the time to meditate.

Clad in brown robes, the bell ringer rose, sat in front of a massive 'singing bowl', arranged his long garment to perfection with movements light and graceful.

He took up the large, padded striker... and paused... and stayed paused... and stayed paused longer... and longer... and even longer.

At the exact moment of highest expectation, he bowed to the bell.

Only then did he, very lightly, strike the rim of the bowl, awakening the bell. Hardly a sound came from the bowl.

Then he paused again... and stayed paused.

He took a breath and struck.

Into the silence rang a tone so pure, the university hall was transformed into a monastery.

In this monastery, the hushed meditators...

learned to listen and to hear the sound of silence.

learned to listen to their breathing.

learned to listen to their restlessness.

learned to listen to the profound teaching of being in each moment... letting go of waiting, letting go of expectation, letting go of wanting.

learned to listen to these lessons that are learned again and again, in every moment.

xxv

A human being would not grow to be seventy or eighty years old if this longevity had no meaning for the species. The afternoon of human life must also have a significance of its own and cannot be merely a pitiful appendage to life's morning.
~~Carl Jung

We can, each of us, take the plunge to the unimagined depths of wisdom in our seventy or eighty years.

We can, each of us, find the meaning for ourselves and for the species in those many decades.

We can, each of us, refuse to be an appendage, worthy of pity.

We can, each of us, find our essential way to embrace our true nature.

We can, each of us, express the authentic self that we are.

We can, each of us, step into our unique power as elders.

For some, this power may be found on the meditation cushion or yoga mat. Here we might find strength and inner resilience. These contemplative practices might provide a haven from the challenges of elderhood as well as a space in which to connect with something greater than ourselves, something we can lean into.

For other elders, this power may manifest in political action, possibly stepping into a new and unfamiliar environment. For others, this arena might be of long acquaintance, with memories of commitments in past decades.

For yet others of us, the power lies in mentoring those younger than we are. They may be in our close circle or those we mentor in literacy or numeracy or in their careers.

Whatever the path to this wisdom might be, each of us can choose to explore, discover or deepen as we walk that road. Unimagined creative expressions of our wisdom and power may arise in our seventies and eighties.

Or we may renew former passions, powerful energies we set aside in our younger years. Regardless of how the path unfolds, each of us has the capacity to find meaning in our elderhood.

We can, each of us, find it in ourselves so that others see and appreciate it.

We can, each of us, embrace the wisdom that is one of the many gifts of our longevity.

We can, each of us, live in the afternoon of life with purpose, joy and significant value.

Opening our hearts to others is a practice taught in many spiritual traditions. It leads to generosity and kindness. It allows us to turn our attention from our self-centred desires and opinions and encourages us to see other perspectives. It softens the fixed and solidified places in our being. It supports our intention to live with compassion, the recognition that all of us experience pain and suffering.

Compassion is one of the qualities of a sage. The sage might live by these words: "With a deep awareness of the suffering of another, coupled with the wish to relieve it, we serve from a deep passion that includes caring and understanding, reciprocity and forgiveness."[iv]

In the Buddhist tradition, the practice of *metta bhavana* is simple and profound. It leads us to a deep awareness of our interconnectedness and affirms our ability to open our heart.

The practice itself asks us to repeat a few simple phrases. The traditional phrases are about happiness, peacefulness and freedom from suffering. Other phrases can be added, of course.

We address these wishes in widening circles. Firstly, we meditate on loving kindness for ourselves. By treating ourselves with the same care, support and kindness we would show a dear friend, we learn compassion for others.

Self-love, which is not the same as selfishness, supports positive change. As we become aware of our own suffering, we are moved to show kindness to others in what we think, say and do.

The second step in the *metta* practice involves holding the phrases for someone we care for deeply, wishing them happiness, peace and freedom.

This is followed by the phrases addressed to a neutral person, someone you might see at the bank or supermarket or on the bus, someone you might barely know or not know at all.

The fourth step of the practice is the most challenging. We practise extending those wishes to someone with whom you are experiencing difficulty – your landlord, a relative, a workmate, your partner. This is where the heart opening is most demanding, and most effective. By asking ourselves to open to someone who we might think is wrong/silly/nasty/stubborn/difficult, we challenge our fixed ideas. We hold our hardened places up to the transformative fire of love and compassion.

Finally, in the last step of *metta bhavana*, we address these wishes to all beings.

The following is the traditional first phase of the practice.

May I be happy.

May I be peaceful.

May I be free from suffering.

Sit in silence, repeating these phrases in your heart-mind for as long as you are comfortable.

In the second step, insert the name of the person you care for in place of 'I', holding an image of that person in your heart.

In the third, address the neutral person, e.g., the postie/the store clerk, holding their image in your heart.

In the fourth step, insert the name of the person with whom you have difficulty, holding that person in your heart.

In the fifth, address all beings, holding the whole planet in your heart.

Again, repeat each of these steps for as long as you are comfortable and then move on to the next one.

May your practice be filled with loving kindness.

~~~

These are some other well-wishes that may be appropriate at various times in your life, as suggested by Sharon Salzberg, a much-loved American Buddhist teacher[v].

May I accept my pain, without thinking it makes me bad or wrong.

May I remember my consciousness is much vaster than this body.

May all beings everywhere be safe, be happy, be peaceful.

May all those who have helped me be safe, be happy, be peaceful.

May my love for myself and others flow boundlessly.

xxvii

The Kabbalistic mystic, Isaac Luria (1534-1572), proposed the practice of *tikkun olam*, healing the world. He believed that when the world began, the Creator formed vessels to hold divine light. Being unable to contain this light, the vessels shattered, still holding a spark of the light trapped in each shard. These shards scattered through the cosmos and formed the world we inhabit.

Luria believed it is the task of humans to reunite these scattered sparks of light and thus repair the broken world.

There is little doubt that our world has shattered. One doesn't need to read the entire newspaper. A glance at the headlines is all we need to convince us that we are in serious trouble. At times, the challenge to be that spark of life seems overwhelming.

In spite of the struggle, we elders might choose to live as if we were exactly the spark of light that is needed to heal the world. We can be a conscious shard. Each day, with our decades of experience, we can contribute something to heal the world we live in.

We might begin with small things... a proverbial act of kindness, planting a tree (or a thousand trees), kissing someone we love, welcoming a refugee, challenging racism and ageism in all its forms.

We each have gifts that heal the world – a smile as you are walking to the shops, a visit to a lonely neighbour, participation in a community art event, mentoring someone who asks for guidance, signing a petition or marching to protect ancient woodlands, standing up for equality, walking a labyrinth with healing intention, a kind word.

Each one of us holds the spark divine light. Each one of us casts that light into the world. No matter how big or small the act, we elders contribute to *tikkun olam*.

May we live today as that spark of light.

xxviii

Our ordinary language calls on us to use the word Reverend to address certain people who have been specially designated as such. We are expected to revere them simply by virtue of their title.

Let's turn the language around so that a reverend is one who reveres, one who respects and honours, one who holds and explores the sacred.

What do I revere?

What do I respect and honour?

What do I hold sacred?

What can I revere each day, in each breath?

Does something have to be designated as 'holy' in order to be revered?

Can I revere the mundane, the ordinary, the usual?

My heart-mind turns to nature each time I contemplate this question. A leaf falling from a branch in autumn... A bud bursting into flower in spring... The cry of a gull... The bounding of a puppy... The grandeur of mountains... The pristine flake of snow... The sound of the sea. All these I revere.

Then my reverence turns to the ordinary events and objects of daily life. A handcrafted bowl... The smile of a passer-by... The joy of my lover's kiss... The miracle of my ageing body... The aroma of brown basmati rice... The comfort of a sofa... The warmth of a winter cardigan... The gift of friendship. All these I revere.

In this way I am reverend.

In this way we who revere are all reverend.

xxix

We live in a culture that asks us to continually add —
possessions, friends, savings, insurance policies. It is as if
we are blank canvases or blank pages, simply waiting to be
filled. At earlier life stages, the only limit was our
imagination. We had energy and drive to splash colours
and write words until, over a lifetime, the page or canvas is
completely covered. What can an elder do with this
metaphoric life painting or completed book? How satisfied
are we with this finished product?

Happy, fulfilled elders are often able to share a secret. At
this period of our lives, we can see ourselves as three-
dimensional, as sculptures. We have not simply been
fortunate to receive the gift of a block of shining Carrara
marble. We were pro-active and sculpted our lives from the
material we were given. With a sure hand on the chisel, we
are now able to rid ourselves of what is no longer
contributing to our lives. We have become sculptures of
awareness and grace, beauty and aliveness.

Elderhood offers the remarkable opportunity to let go, to
strip away all that distracts us from the process of
deepening consciousness, all that clouds our ability to be
fully in the now. We can find the energy to release outworn
ideas and contribute our long unused paraphernalia to
charity. Thus, we make space to refine our inner
possessions as well as our outer environment.

We then become the beings we were meant to be, the

embodiment hidden in the marble block. Having let go of the objects and opinions, even beliefs, that have held us back for decades, we become more spacious, freer. Suddenly, we are living a life of meaning where we express each aspect of ourselves authentically.

As a sculptor sees the finished work in the raw block of marble, we release, unveiling our true self into the world. We become inspiring beings, beautiful in our elderhood, free of what is peripheral to the truth of who we are.

Happiness can now radiate from us as stunning works of our own creativity. We have become living, breathing sculptures, affirming our commitment to the joy of elderhood.

xxx

Skin, that thinnest of coverings, envelopes us completely from month four *in utero*. From that time on, we are encased in just over half an inch of skin, 22 square feet, 8 pounds of it. Not much separating us from the rest of the world. Not much between you and me, and her and him, and them and us. Just half an inch.

Easily bruised, sliced, banged, cut, gashed, slashed, scored, incised, lacerated, wounded in all manner of ways by all manner of things, we bathe it, exfoliate it, cream it, oil it, shave it, in the vain attempt to keep it as it was – smooth, silky, burnished, flawless, unwrinkled. Especially unwrinkled. Unscarred by the experiencing life. Unmarred by love and death. Unscathed by time passing. Unmarked by breath, tears, sweat, heartbeat. Untorn by incident, event, adventure, affair or circumstance.

Not long ago, I noticed the tender skin on the underside of my forearm. Not the bones. Not the soon-to-be swollen joints. Just the skin. There was a visible pattern of lines and spaces that looked familiar, though I couldn't place it.

About once a week, I looked again at the same arm and, fascinated, saw the same pattern. Was it alligator skin? Was it parchment? Was it elephant hide?

On a sunny day at the seashore, with the tide receding off the golden sand, the sea racing away from the dunes, there it was. I saw my skin, the skin of sand, the skin of the planet.

Engraved in ever-changing grains was the pattern, striated, barred, banded, streaked, like a fern or a feather. Like an old woman's skin.

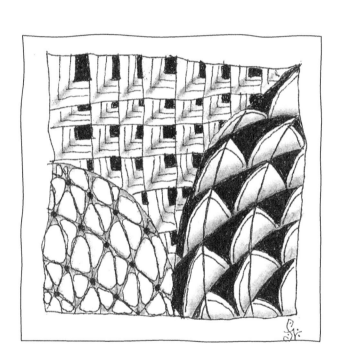

xxxi

Small things surround us, everyday things. We may find these small things in aspects of the natural world – bees, tiny flowers miraculously growing in the cracks of a wall or pavement, fluttering leaves. Focusing on small things, we may see our home with different eyes – a cushion, a table, a photograph. We may even find these small things in our friends – their smile, their tears. Though we might see less in quantity, we create the environment in which to see deeply in quality.

This fine-focused looking enables us to nurture a deep sense of appreciation and gratitude. Cultivating a sense of wonder at the small, simple things opens a door to the infinite, the world in a drop of water. Wonder is often seen as the domain of the young. We too can choose to live in this miraculous world, filled infinitely with the new, the unexplored. Our elder world thus becomes wonder-full.

With awareness of the small things, our consciousness shifts to a different lens. Younger times saw many of us with big dreams of changing the world. (And we did!) Now, with decades behind us, we can see the immensity of each small thing, each small step. Elders have learned from experience – big, and especially small.

Gratitude, regardless of our circumstances, allows us to hold those small things in right relationship to our inner and outer being. They can create the bridge between you and me, between us and them, between life and death.

Take a moment to stop and look keenly at a small thing. Breathe with it. Hold it, in your hand or in your heart. Embrace it. Let it speak to you of its being, of its creation.

Listen with the ears of your heart to the small things, the symphony of being.

Look at less, see more deeply.

xxxii

As our days pass, some flow with ease, others don't. There are days of glorious sunrises, delightful adventures, deep connections and great telly. Other days bring regret, leaden skies, anxiety, painful news and boredom.

We live days that remind us clearly of the passage of time in our physical self. An injury, a twist, a shooting pain, another limitation. These are the days that we might find ourselves in a feedback loop of sensation, labelling, desire for relief, ice packs and over-the-counter pain killers. Sometimes, when we do 'good' things such as exercise, we discover these challenges. They just seem to happen, out of the blue, out of our life on planet Earth. Sometimes there is no discernible cause, sometimes a very clear cause.

The entire gamut of emotions often arises in these moments: anger, disbelief, fury, amazement, sadness, grief, curiosity.

Curiosity might fascinate the elder and lead to inner inquiry. How has my body changed? Do I need to visit a health care practitioner? My GP? A&E? What can I learn from this new ache, this unexpected pain, this 'different' body? Where is my threshold for these changes? Can I breathe through this?

'Curiosity seasoned with discernment' might be the mantra of our ageing body. Buddhists suggest we sit with and observe the sensations in the knowledge that they will change. The sensations will increase, decrease, cease altogether. Change they will. Decades of experience in our body has taught us the ways in which we usually open to the new, and how we often shut down to the unexpected, and what actions we ordinarily take. As elders, we can learn to approach these inevitable changes with compassion for ourselves and our peers, and then take appropriate action.

Some days are easy, some days are not. What is important is self-knowledge. We know our patterns and can choose to follow them, or to try something different. Willingness to explore the new allows us to grow into elderhood, just as it allowed us to grow into adulthood.

One path is not better than another, simply different. It is self-awareness that matters, regardless of whether the day is easy, or not.

xxxiii

Many of our lives are no longer filled with the hurry of a job, the endless appointments and commitments, the worry of impressing others, the angst of wondering who we are and what are we doing with our lives.

Now we have time and space to be, to surrender doing in favour of being.

What does that mean, really? Most of us were not taught how to be, only how to do and accomplish. The vast majority of us were not raised in an idealised, spiritually focused household. In fact, quite the opposite. And yet, somehow, we can learn to be. We can learn that this moment, and the next moment, and the next moment, are all we truly have. We can learn to be, in the present.

All our possessions are transitory, the odds and ends of the past. Many are precious to us, though we know they will eventually decay, find their way to a charity shop, end up in landfill or on a friend's mantlepiece until she too dies. Some family heirlooms may be gifted on for a few more generations, but little else will survive the passing of time.

Time itself cannot be in this present moment. Time itself exists only as the past and the future. It cannot destroy the next present moment. Nor is there a place for this moment in landfill. Nor will it be inherited by our descendants. Each moment can only be experienced in the richness of our unique internal state of being.

In the state of now, there is space for every experience to be truly felt and integrated. Each moment-to-moment awareness creates a new bit of life wisdom that can be shared, passed on, given away. This is the spirit of eldering. This is the gift of decades of learning, of transforming, of loving life... moment by moment, experience by experience, breath by breath.

This internal richness, the fruit of our life's labours, is this golden treasure of being – and of being an elder.

xxxiv

One recent morning I encountered a neighbour who I rarely see. I commented that I was glad to see her. She's very busy, so these meetings don't come often. She attends Spanish and French classes, as well an exercise class, several times each week. It was a Wednesday, the day there is a weekly social club in a spacious, well-appointed community space near where we live. The neighbour asked me if I attended. When I said: "No," she commented, "Nor do I. They think they're old. I don't think I'm old."

What is it about the word 'old' that causes us to recoil, to distance ourselves from others, to reject our peers? Why do we dread claiming that identity? In our culture, old means useless, without redeeming qualities. My neighbour's response to a vital community activity typifies our current cultural reality and the prevailing paradigm of ageing.

Perhaps, more importantly, she is denying her own reality. Though I don't know exactly how old she is, I imagine she has 75 or more years of life experience. That's old by anyone's standards, including the biblical 'three score and ten'. She is healthy, engaged, useful, lively. And old.

We have been conditioned to believe that young is valuable, desirable. We who are no-longer-young are not. They who are not-yet-old inhabit a world that is often bereft of elder role models. They don't yet know the potential freedom of elderhood. They don't yet know the avenues for growth that exist in the lives of those of us who are older than they are.

Most research shows that people in their later years are happier and more content that those younger. We somehow believe the young and middle years are the epitome of life's riches, the decades of greatest happiness. Current studies show otherwise[vi].

Nevertheless, the cultural view of 'old' persists. It is up to us to change that – by living our potential regardless of our age, by enjoying opportunities for growth, by finding meaning and purpose in our elderhood itself.

By being old.

xxxv

In both yoga and Buddhist traditions, we encounter the interdependent opposites of *sukha* and *dukkha*. The Taoists called them yin and yang.

Sukha is the root of the English word 'sugar'. This is the sweet time of life, the moments when everything just works. It all fits together. There is joy and laughter, sunshine and starlight.

Dukkha expresses the polar opposite: pain, misery, anxiety. This is the difficult time of life when nothing flows. Nothing fits. There are tears and groans, grey days and sleepless nights.

This is the stuff of our human condition.

Yogis have a perfect image for this polarity, the wheel. When the axle holding the wheel is bent or broken, the wheel can't turn. When the rim of the wheel is out of true, it bumps on the road. When the hub is misaligned, we experience a rough ride, *dukkha*.

If the rim is perfectly circular, and the hub sits comfortably on a strong and straight axle, the ride of life is smooth and effortless. We are in the sweet spot, *sukha*.

In the classic *Yoga Sutra*, the wise elder Patanjali wrote, "S*thira sukam asanam*," meaning "the posture (how we are in the world) is steady and comfortable". The wheel is true. We sit sweetly in comfort and strength.

Elderhood requires both steadiness and comfort, strength and flexibility. We take our place with ease and assuredness. We become wisdom keepers. When we guide younger people along their chosen path, we sit in our comfort and strength. When we have meaningful conversation with our peers, we are comfortable, honouring their wisdom as well as our own.

The flexibility we have learned supports us as we negotiate the turbulence of world affairs with kindness and compassion. We have experienced both *sukha* and *dukkha*, bringing both to our eldering. The wheel turns with ease on the hub. The rim too rolls gently, in sure contact with the ground.

Our spiritual connection, whatever it might be, maintains the health of the wheel. This connection is our mechanic at the garage of our inner self, ready to oil and adjust and align so we can live in *sukha*, the sweet spot, and with a minimum of suffering, *dukkha*.

It is vital to our life – as elders.

It enables us to be fully authentic and alive – as elders.

xxxvi

In yoga practice, the heart centre is called *anahata*. *Anahata* means the sound that is made without striking one thing upon another, as with a stick or mallet on a drum or gong. It is regarded as the sound of the celestial realm and holds balance, calm and tranquillity. This is a space where we can connect with ourselves, with others, and with spirit. That sound, like so much of our inner lives, is ineffable and cannot readily be expressed in words.

And yet we know what we mean when we speak of the heart. The heart, in many western cultures, is often regarded as the seat of emotion. Warm-hearted people are attractive, drawing us to them. The opposite is true of those who might be regarded as cold-hearted.

As we live into our elder years, the heart can also hold fear... Heart attack looming? Pacemaker? High blood pressure? Coronary artery disease? Valve replacement? Cancer and heart disease are now in a close race for the dubious honour of number one killer, with cancer just beginning to overtake heart disease. In the UK, more women die of heart disease than breast cancer.

While we might have concerns about our hearts, the organ itself is filled with wonder.

Every day, the average human heart beats around 70 times per minute – 100,000 beats per day.

Though it's a muscle, it never gets fatigued.

It will beat more than 2.5 billion times by the time we are 70.

Our blood travels 19,000 km every day – the equivalent of London to Hong Kong and back.

It pumps 7,200 litres of blood every day.[vii]

Alongside this amazing muscle lives the *anahata,* the space of tranquillity and balance. We can foster calm with each heartbeat, with each 'unstruck sound'. We can connect with the celestial realm with contemplative practices, such as meditation or Qigong/Ch'i Kung. We can care for our physical heart with appropriate exercise, diet and medical care. At the same time, we can cultivate and nurture inner peace.

Each day will, no doubt, bring its share of joy and challenges as our years progress. The heart-space remains constant and unchanging. The *anahata,* the space of the celestial realm, rings its unstuck sound with each heartbeat. It is with us at all times, always available.

We need only remember the sound.

xxxvii

There is an open invitation to take a journey to visit the temple of memory.

In this temple, everything is sacred. Failings and successes, mistakes and accomplishments, regrets and joys all live together in this numinous space. We can awaken here and hold all that we have experienced in eternal space. In this hallowed hall, the joys and the connections live alongside the memories of sadness and grief. Each memory embellishes the temple like a rose in full bloom, its scent an enchantment.

Here we can offer the harvest of a lifetime, available on deep reflection, and give meaning and depth to all we have experienced. In the cherished place of contemplation, of stillness, we gather in the riches of living. Then, we can honour ourselves and step into elderhood. We become the vessel for wisdom and can create a legacy for those who follow us on their unique journey. They may be younger than we are, or they may be our peers, our companions on the path to the temple.

Conversations can be held on the doorstep of the temple; within, guidance can be given and received. Yet each of us must enter the temple of memory alone. Each solitary step takes us deeper into the plenitude of our life. Each solitary step brings us into the sanctuary of greater understanding, greater compassion and greater generosity. Each solitary step brings us into connection with others as they experience their own temple.

We can leave markers that lead to the door of the temple of memory, marking the way for others. In this way, we share together, in community, the awakening into elderhood.

xxxviii

"I don't have time."
"It's too late."
"It isn't the same as it was before."
"Life is short."
"I'm too old."
"I could never do that."
"Time marches on."

The sense of time is deeply ingrained in language. We usually see it as linear and unambiguous – you're born, you live, and then you die. There will certainly be shifts along the road when time 'stood still', when time was 'wasted', when it 'flew by'. Nevertheless, we tend to think of time marching in a procession of minutes, hours, days, months and years.

Theoretical physicist Carlo Rovelli tells us that "Time is a fascinating topic because it touches our deepest emotions. Time opens up life and takes everything away. Wondering about time is wondering about the very sense of our life."[viii]

The passage of time pervades our awareness as we grow into elderhood and note the seemingly inevitable changes. We see changes in our appearance and respond with sadness or curiosity, or perhaps a bit of both. We enjoy each year's celebrations and wonder how many more we will live to enjoy.

Yet physicists tell us there is no time; there are only events.

A stone might seem like an unchanging thing. Scientists declare it is really an event moving so slowly in time we can't register it. The stone itself is in constant transformation, moving on a long journey to something else, taking place over time.

As we open our hearts to the long journey we have lived, we might see our own unfolding as so many events taking place at various speeds throughout our life. Events of our childhood may still be reverberating in us today, moving slowly on the path to something else. The memory of an adventure in a tree house might become a thoughtful musing decades later, a tingle of that remembered joy retained in today's body-mind. A pain today might transform into a poem that takes years to write. We might have recently learned a new skill that leads us into an exciting adventure, undreamed in earlier time.

Re-viewing, looking again, allows us to appreciate the events that we are now and how we have been transformed. Some events were turning points, places where time shifted and we became something else.

Which event of being will reveal itself in this moment – in time?

xxxix

"I used to be able to…"

How often in conversation does this phrase occur?

Most likely, we each have a list of answers…

When I was younger, I used to be able to…

touch my toes
get up from the floor with ease
open a jar of mayonnaise
walk miles at a good clip
enjoy hours of driving
work 10 hours in a day
dance until the wee hours
mow the lawn and pull weeds
lift a child almost thoughtlessly
read small print
never think about catching a cold
enjoy a loud concert
remember names and faces

An alternative list

When I was younger, I was unable to...

mentor people younger than I am

sit quietly, simply because I want to

enjoy a leisurely stroll on the seafront

listen deeply to another's joy or anguish

share ideas that spring from my heart

turn the light off when I'm tired

notice the tiny flower growing in a crack in the pavement

enjoy learning something new simply for its own sake

connect deeply with my inner self

read books solely for pleasure

challenge myself to grow

apologise gracefully when I forget a name

make room for more wisdom as the non-essentials fall away

share my life's experience

understand my worth

accept the errors in judgement and the pain I caused

learn the lessons of successes and failures

xl

Knowing at the time of our death that we have been as true to ourselves as we could be offers deep spiritual comfort. The honoured Quaker teacher and author Parker Palmer also reminds us that his deepest pain is knowing that he might have "rarely, if ever, shown up as my true self."[ix]

Our inner being, conscious or not, knows who and what that true self is. Our elder years offer us the gateway to expressing this truth. We can step through the gate and discover, moment by moment, the life that lies ahead. We are then guided by our true self.

Or we can continue to simply walk the familiar, comfortable, well-trodden avenues of the past, guided by habit and the expectations of others.

With our mortality ever-present, now is the time to live into our truth. For some, this exploration may be well-known from years of inquiry and meditation. For those less familiar with contemplative practices, now is the time to dive into the profound bedrock of who we are.

Faith traditions have various names for this truth. Hindus call it *atman*. For Buddhists, it is our *Buddha nature*. Christians name it *Holy Spirit*. You may have a personal name for that unchanging, stable essence of yourself, that still centre that remains calm when the world around you spins out through chaos.

How much more comforting, on our death bed, to know we

have lived a life of authenticity, integrity, and candour. We will then find ourselves open to love, and able to receive the gifts of our last moments, our final breaths. The dying of the physical self may not be easy, though our minds and hearts can be at ease knowing that we have lived from our true self.

xli

As we take some time for contemplation, we might wonder about the proverbial meaning of life. We've lived six, seven or eight decades. What does it all mean?

One wise man, Joseph Campbell, wrote, "People say that what we're all seeking is a meaning for life ... I think that what we're seeking is an experience of being alive, so that our life experiences on the purely physical plane will have resonances with our own innermost being and reality, so that we actually feel the rapture of being alive."[x]

The desire to feel that inner resonance continues throughout a life span. In our elderhood, we have time to make that connection between our outer, physical life and our inner being – that still, small voice that dwells in each of us. We now have the opportunity to live this inner core, our deepest truth. When that connection is made, we can, in Campbell's well-known words, follow our bliss.

Then each day, each breath, is experienced in its fullest meaning. Each tear that is shed carries the joy and the grief of decades. Each smile holds all the moments of gladness as well as the moments of embarrassment and shyness. Each sob holds the truth of experience along with each peal of laughter. Each moment of irritation or frustration embraces the moments of deep satisfaction.

In spite of the difficulty of putting this ineffable experience into solid words, it is this sense of aliveness, of deep connection with self, that Campbell so eloquently expressed. We all know those moments of aliveness – a stunning sunset, a tender kiss from a beloved one, a moment when our heart broke open, a compassionate encounter. As elders, we have a huge archive of these experiences. They are the rapture of being alive.

Another wise man, Stephen Hawking, reminds us that "It matters that you don't just give up."[xi] Giving up is the antithesis of the experience of aliveness. It defeats our desire for the enchantment of true connection. Hawking was certainly the expert at 'not giving up'. His life had meaning, just as does each of our lives.

Alive with meaning, vibrating with the energy of life, we continue to grow and evolve into our elderhood.

xlii

Who am I to be an elder? What wisdom do I have? Who would look up to me? I don't hold the stories of my supposed tribe! The term 'elder' may bring up these and other reactions in your heart-mind.

In many Indigenous cultures, older people are expected to use their wisdom, gathered from long experience, in ways that will guide and benefit their communities. They become the community's leaders. This transition often happens at age 50(!). The elders take on this mantle and thus participate fully in the life of their community, rather than simply becoming invisible and waiting to die.

Very few of us live in this tribal way, though our family, whether of blood or choice, could be seen as a tribe. Many of us at 50 are still working and in the 'adult' phase of life. We move into elderhood much later these days.

The question, for us, remains: what differentiates an 'elder' from an 'older' in our society? The answer is multi-dimensional. Being willing to 'assume the mantle' of an elder indicates a change in consciousness. Internally, we step over a threshold in the heart. We recognise our unique experience and its value to those around us.

We also become aware that the work of the adult phase has, for the most part, ended and the tasks of the elder phase begun. Though we may still be in the world of livelihood, our vision of the world has changed, along with our relationship to it.

This change of consciousness doesn't automatically happen with the accumulation of years. It is the result of inner transformation that comes from looking deeply at that which needs healing, re-framing, nurturing, forgiving and preparing. Transformed, we can live in the harvest and celebration of our authenticity, of who we truly are.

While not every older may be an elder right now, all olders have the inner potential to become elders. As we change our consciousness, we become more honest, more courageous and open. In this process we willingly, and with great kindness, take the challenging step to explore our mortality. This inner inquiry, somewhat counter-intuitively, allows us to laugh, to find joy and to live each day to the full. We can live our values with more zest. We can see life at its juicy best!

xliii

The question is not simply what should we do about [our collective] problems. The larger question is ...
who do we have to become in order to solve them?
~~Marianne Williamson, *The Politics of Love*

We have, at any moment, the opportunity to become different, to be the beings we aspire to become. This is our moment. Times of catastrophe, like the pandemic of 2020, can be pivotal moments of transformation. There have been catastrophes and plagues in the past. Many times, the human community has risen to those occasions and transformed cultures and societies.

Each year in spring, Jewish communities around the world celebrate Passover, the festival of freedom from slavery. In the story we find an enslaved people liberated by the coming of plagues. There was blood raining from the sky, and locusts, boils and frogs. The journey from slavery to freedom was not easy. Those who were born into and lived their lives in slavery had to face the challenge of crossing the Sea of Reeds. Then they wandered in the desert long enough for the generation of slaves to die before reaching their promised land – freedom.

How can we, as elders, find liberation for ourselves so that we might lead others to freedom in a time of limitation and challenge? What have we experienced that will provide strength to those who are weakened, courage to those who are frightened, and comfort to those who are distressed?

What plagues have we survived? What shackles of slavery have we thrown off?

We have learned that, in the biggest picture, the Earth will keep turning, as we see flowers and leaves emerge in the spring. We have learned that the suffering and death of those we love can be grieved and enfolded into the richness of who we are. We know that an open heart, filled with love and compassion, can provide a beacon in the dark times. We can take action, however small, from that compassionate heart to relieve the suffering of others and begin to solve the problems presented to us.

At the same time as we hold others, we are eldering ourselves... and being who we aspire to be.

xliv

Frank Ostaseski founded the San Francisco Zen Hospice in 1987 in response to the AIDS crisis in the United States. From people who were living their dying days, he learned five vital lessons for living. He invites us to pay attention to these five invitations for flourishing now, with deep awareness of our ageing and inevitable dying.[xii]

(This, and the next four contemplations, explore his insights and are best read in order.)

We are first invited to 'Don't wait.'

This invitation, contrary to popular thinking, is not about a 'to-do' list, or the dreaded bucket list of things we are told by others to accomplish before we die. When we 'don't wait', we live each moment with the profound knowledge that each one will pass, like all things.

When we 'don't wait', we might find that some meaningless activities fall by the wayside, to be replaced by those that nourish us. Our focus becomes laser-like, taking us deeper into what sustains us. Heartfelt desires from long ago might arise in answer to this invitation, having been put aside when we were younger in response to more immediate needs. Now, as we 'don't wait', is their time to bear fruit.

Hardened opinions might become more fluid. When we 'don't wait', a willingness to listen to others arises in the space between us so we can explore into a deeper truth.

Our very identities might suddenly become less defined and limited because we occupy the now, moving us away from who we were in the past.

As we focus consciously on the present, as it is, right now, right here, we are released from the longing for some better future. We know the 'now' is all we truly have. In the space of 'don't wait', we live fully, knowing that each moment living into our true nature creates the next moment.

Zen Master Suzuki Roshi suggests we develop *constancy*, "... a capacity to be with what is true, moment after moment."

Ostaseski tells us, "Don't wait is a pathway to fulfilment and an antidote to regret."

xlv

Contemplations xliv to xlviii are best read in order, beginning with xliv (page 118).

The second invitation on this list may be even more challenging. 'Welcome everything, push nothing away.' It is helpful to remember that this list was written by someone working in the crucible of pain, dying and death. Yet Ostaseski reminds us that it is possible to welcome even all of that.

This welcoming is an invitation to become more open, more spacious, with a curious, wakeful mind. This mind lives in the current reality. This invitation asks us to look at whatever arises and be with it as part of a larger process. In this expanded space, we let go of any attachment to our particular view of how things should be.

This responsive view is the very nature of awareness. It permits contradiction and paradox at the same time as our heart opens to receive new experiences and information. In this state we can tolerate the unknown, the beautiful and the sordid, the moments of pleasure and the moments of pain as equally valid experiences.

In this openness we move toward, lean into what is, as it is. We may not have asked for it, or like it, or want it, or agree with it. In those moments, we might remember that when we fight with reality, we lose every time, exhausting ourselves arguing with it in the hope that life might be different than it is.

By living in the truth of what actually presents itself to us, we live an authentic, passionate life, filled with vibrance and potential.

xlvi

Contemplations xliv to xlviii are best read in order,
beginning with xliv (page 118).

Midway through Ostaseski's invitations, we find, 'Bring your whole self to the experience.'

Whenever we can, we approach life from our best self, the place inside that is complete and integrated. We endeavour to look good and to be seen as caring, capable, attractive, intelligent, sensitive and moderately well-balanced.

We just as certainly don't want to appear helpless, angry, fearful or ignorant. We don't want to appear to be a mess, ever! Not even when we are ageing and dying!

Our whole self, of course, includes what we might deem to be undesirable, ugly, unworthy of attention, even horrific. These are the bits that are often hidden away in the dark corners of our selves. These are the parts of us that are covered in shame and fear. We are terrified they might pop up at any moment, unbidden, embarrassing and possibly mortifying.

This invitation asks us to bring all of it – our anger, our fear, our uncertainty and our shame along with the joy and freedom – to the experiences we have as we grow older. In this way, we can be honest with ourselves and with those around us. Awareness of our shadow, our hidden side, allows our ageing to be whole, as the shadow sits alongside our light.

As we grow older, we have the opportunity to explore all parts of ourselves, including the shadow. Here we find not only the parts we deemed 'bad', but the parts that allow us to set appropriate boundaries, our place of personal power and emotional intelligence. As we accept our wholeness, we can accept others in their wholeness. Our relationships deepen and our compassion flourishes.

Bringing all of ourselves to each moment makes visible our authenticity and integrity. We are real, in our own eyes and in the eyes of the world around us.

xlvii

Contemplations xliv to xlviii are best read in order, beginning with xliv (page 118).

We are now invited to 'Find a place of rest in the middle of things.' We might imagine that rest comes from changing our outer circumstances: when we've ticked everything off our to-do list, go on holiday, had a massage, gotten a pay rise, or when our partner agrees with our point of view.

This invitation asks us to find an <u>inner</u> place of rest, one that exists regardless of the circumstances around us. That said, we need to acknowledge that some conditions are simply unacceptable, and that outer change needs to happen. Finding the place of inner rest supports us in finding what we need, and what outer actions we must take.

The place of inner rest is always available, even in our dying process. We can aspire to turn toward it, lean into the calm of the resting place. Perhaps we might see it as a choice we make, even in the midst of a storm. It is a choice to be awake, to be alert, to attend to this moment.

This is the space of full attention on this moment, on this activity, on this event. As we deepen our response to this invitation, we come to recognise this rest space as an aspect of awareness.

This peace is the internal Sabbath that can be found on any day of the week. We can discover it in each moment when we honour the truth of the present – even in those moments of wanting the present to be different, or regret, or anger, or pain. Even in those moments when we experience our deepest fear.

This rest is always available; it's never ill, out to lunch, or on Zoom. It is unborn and it is undying, always present and available. In Ostaseski's words, "Awareness itself is our ultimate resting place."

xlviii

*Contemplations xliv to xlviii are best read in order,
beginning with xliv (page 118).*

The last invitation asks us to 'Cultivate don't know mind.'
This is the mind that embraces curiosity and wonder. It is
open, and can receive what shows up for us, exactly as it is
and exactly as we are.

'Don't know mind' is not the same as ignorance. It is not
lack of information or knowledge or experience. Nor is it
the wilful turning away from facts.

'Don't know mind' is beyond knowing or not knowing. It is
what Suzuki Roshi so famously called 'beginner's mind'.
This is the mind, he taught us, that holds many
possibilities, while the expert's mind holds very few. The
expert already knows everything.

'Don't know mind' has no limits or boundaries. It has no
expectations and is willing to simply be. It has no roles or
agendas. It is not fixed into a position and remains willing
and thoughtful. Inquisitive and intrigued, this mind allows
us to be compassionate and humble because we know that
we don't know.

Whatever is present for us has never been experienced
before, so how can we know or predict the outcome? It
might be that we are facing a thorny problem, or we are
building a relationship, or we are completing a project. By
bringing a mind guided by interest and presence, along

with our experience and knowledge, we can let go of control. We can approach the present moment with a mind that is open. We can then enter life, even in our last moments, with an open heart. We can relax into the present, realising that our true nature is spacious and boundless and flowing in the ever-changing river of continual change.

These five invitations serve as a guide as we age with awareness, allowing us to deepen into living our elderhood with vitality and tranquillity, with curiosity and resilience.

xlix

sagacity, sageness, intelligence, understanding, insight,
perception, perceptiveness, percipience, perspicuity,
acuity, discernment, sense, good sense, common sense,
shrewdness, astuteness, acumen, smartness,
judiciousness, judgement, foresight, clear-sightedness,
prudence, circumspection

Each of those words has a sense of spiritual understanding, of gravitas, of respect. These are qualities we have been told are inherent in older people. Are they? Does one gain acumen or discernment simply by living into one's sixth, seventh or eighth decade? Do we acquire common sense or prudence by living by someone else's rule book, following the advice to increase the amount in our savings account and 'make arrangements'?

How can we express our wisdom, our experience, our knowledge in a society that blames us both for creating the 'mess' we're in and for holding back those younger than we are? How does our foresight influence others who are planning for the future? Where is our insight called upon when, somehow, it seems to be all our fault?

The truth is hard to find. In spite of the blaming headlines, we are still a minority. (The number of people aged 65 years and over is expected to increase by 1.6% over 2021-22 to total 12.7 million, accounting for only 18.9% of the total UK population, though it is the highest proportion this age group has ever comprised.)

Our age is not the problem, just as gender, skin colour, or sexual preference are not the problem.

Ageism is the problem, just as sexism/racism/homophobia are the problem.

Ageism, also called age discrimination, occurs when someone treats another person unfairly because of their age. It can also include the way that older people are represented in the media, which has a serious impact on cultural attitudes. Ageism has a negative effect on self-worth and self-perception, employment and economic status, health care and quality of life.

We can learn from the successes other minorities have achieved over the last few decades. We can bring our true wisdom – our foresight and discernment, our acumen and understanding – to bear on the creation of a new paradigm for our own ageing and the inevitable ageing of those younger than we are, whether they know it yet or not.

l

In a recent conversation, a dear friend commented about the lack of spirituality in her life. She said that over the decades she used to meditate, write poetry, sing and write music. Then she went on to tell me about all that she had been doing recently – tirelessly working with people who are unhoused, actively supporting children in Africa, caring for her grandson and his canine friends.

A word popped out of my mouth as I reminded her about all this activity. I told her I was certain she did all these things as an 'enspirited' elder. I'm not sure I created this word, though I smiled as it tumbled through my lips. This new word must have connected to 'enthused' in my mind. 'Enthuse' took a linguistic journey from Greek *enthusiasmous* to Late Latin *enthusiasmus* to 16th century French *enthousiasme* to the English word we know today. In all those languages it meant 'filled with divine inspiration'. To be enthusiastic about something gives us the inspiration and energy to carry it out, to live it, to be it.

An enspirited life cannot be measured by how often we sit on the meditation cushion, nor how many times we attend a religious service, nor how many yoga classes we frequent. It can, however, be experienced in our connection – to ourselves, to others, to the planet and to something that transcends.

To be enspirited is to be fully present with whatever is in the moment.

To be enspirited is to be alive to each passing breath, each passing thought, each passing step, each passing sensation.

To be enspirited is to be with each emotion.

To be enspirited is to live and to love.

This enspirited life can define our days as conscious elders, as we embody spiritual eldering in all that we do. We now have the time and space to create such a life and to live it with full enthusiasm, filled with inspiration.

li

One of the many qualities of wisdom and wise people is wonder. The wise ones, embracing wonder, standing in awe, are led to great humility. A wise one, with the eyes of the eagle, sees the vastness of life and its unfathomable mystery and can only stand in the wonder of it all. The wise ones never proclaim themselves as wise.

The ego of the wise ones is smaller than their ability to simply model humility and wonder.

The energetic tension between the vastness of creation and the modest space we occupy can fill us with delight. It can open the heart-mind to the electricity of the life force that is called *prana* in Sanskrit, *qi/chi* in Chinese, *ki* in Japanese. Welcoming this pulse of life is a hallmark of an elder.

Elders, in the course of our growth, can surrender to this greater energy. We then find ourselves in a state of amazement. There seems to be a circular relationship between humility and wonder. The more we can open to the astonishing world around us, the more we see ourselves as a small, yet integral part of an unbounded whole.

This creative tension allows an elder to also appreciate the interdependent dynamic between joy and grief, between anger and resolution, between sadness and gladness, between laughter and tears, between rage and compassion, between past experience and the present moment. Intimate knowledge of each aspect of the life force can bring the elder to a fundamental understanding: each aspect is vital to life itself.

To embrace the parts of ourselves that are painful along with the parts that bring peace allows us to welcome our wholeness, living in the cycle of wonder and humility, the rhythmic nature of all life.

lii

Sometimes you have to do things you don't want to do.

Most of us have spent quite a long time doing what we might not *want* to do: unfulfilling jobs, parent care, childcare, endless meetings, trying holidays with family, dealing with challenging relationships, living through losses of varying magnitude, learning lots of difficult lessons.

We've all had to, over the decades, face fierce teachers and teachings. We've all had to, over the decades, sacrifice our desires for something we thought was more important or more valuable. We've all had to, over the decades, suffer pain, discomfort, illnesses... none of which we wanted or chose.

Now, as elders in the present, we may continue to do things we don't *want* to do. Now, however, as elders in the present, we can make those choices more consciously. With more time to reflect, to look inside for our truth, we can choose to go ahead with what we don't *want* to do... or we can say "no".

We can choose to do the things and activities that nourish us and let go of the things and activities that don't.

Yes, we might miss out on something entertaining.

Yes, we might forego an opportunity.

Yes, we might pass up something unknown.

Yes, someone's feelings may be hurt... and we will deal with the consequences.

Yes, we can choose to listen to the deep, inner voice that says "no".

Yes, we can save our energy for that which is exciting, challenging, energising, invigorating, creative, loving, compelling.

Yes, we can make choices that might have seemed impossible without the wisdom and experience we have gained over the decades. We have harvested that wisdom after facing the challenges, and we can now act from a place of inner strength.

We can, as elders in the present, say "yes", <u>and</u> we can say "no".

Epigraph

"My father, who lived to 94, often said that the 80s had been one of the most enjoyable decades of his life. He felt, as I begin to feel, not a shrinking but an enlargement of mental life in perspective. One has had a long experience of life, not only one's own life, but others too. One has seen triumphs and tragedies, booms and busts, revolutions and wars, great achievements and deep ambiguities. One has seen grand theories rise, only to be toppled by stubborn facts. One is more conscious of transience and, perhaps, of beauty. At 80, one can take a long view and have a vivid lived sense of history not possible at an earlier age. I can imagine, feel in my bones, what a century is like, which I could not do when I was 40 or 60."

~~Oliver Sacks (1933-2015), from his essay *Mercury*, written a few days before his 80th birthday.

Further Reading

From Age-ing to Sage-ing: A Revolutionary Approach to Growing Older
>Zalman Schachter-Shalomi and Ronald S Miller

The Five Invitations: Discovering What Death Can Teach Us About Living Fully
>Frank Ostaseski

Living an Examined Life: Wisdom for the Second Half of the Journey
>James Hollis, Ph.D.

This Chair Rocks: A Manifesto Against Ageism
>Ashton Applewhite

What Does It Feel Like to Die?: Inspiring New Insights into the Experience of Dying
>Jennie Dear

Japanese Death Poems
>ed. Yoel Hoffman

Breaking the Age Code
>Dr Becca Levy

A Matter of Death and Life: Love, Loss and What Matters in the End
>Irvin D Yalom and Marilyn Yalom

Elderhood: Redefining Aging, Transforming Medicine, Reimagining Life
    Louise Aronson

Conscious Living, Conscious Aging: Embrace & Savor Your Next Chapter
    Ron Pevny

With the End in Mind: How to Live and Die Well
    Kathryn Mannix

Healing into Life and Death
    Stephen Levine

The Book About Getting Older
    Dr Lucy Pollock

Gratitude

With a deep bow of gratitude to Beatrice Ammidown, Janey Verney and Clive Johnson for their mindful and sensitive readings of the very rough outlines of these contemplations. Their feedback and suggestions were invaluable.

With a bow that becomes a hug to my niece and nephew, Elena and Jonathan, for the gifts that blood family can provide.

With a joyous bow of gratitude to the London Writers Salon and the hundreds of writers who gather several times a day, across the globe, to write together and to form a community of creative souls.

With a delighted bow of gratitude to Sage-ing International and the hundreds of elders and elders-in-training who gather, across the globe, in webinars, live workshops, wisdom circles and friendship networks to embody elderhood. Special thanks to Jerome Kerner, Rosemary Cox and Jeanne Marsh.

With a reverential bow to all my teachers – spiritual, academic, yogic, practical, creative – who have taught me life lessons that continue to guide my exploration and transformation. Special thanks to Sally Kempton, Joseph LePage, and the many inter-connected circles of the OneSpirit Interfaith Foundation.

With a smiling bow of decades-long friendship to Jo

Palumbo, who started it all.

With a humble bow of respect to Alison Thompson – publication guru, editorial sleuth, ever-present champion – for her compassionate professional support. (www.theprooffairy.com)

References

[i] www.charlottewattshealth.co.uk

[ii] www.discovermagazine.com/planet-earth/20-things-you-didn%27t-know-about-crystals

[iii] The Jewish sacred text

[iv] Sage-ing International (www.sage-ing.org)

[v] www.yogajournal.com/meditation/cultivate-goodness-practice-lovingkindness

[vi] time.com/collection/guide-to-happiness/4464811/aging-happiness-stress-anxiety-depression/

[vii] *The Surgeon Who Fell in Love with Broken Hearts*, The I Newspaper,
12 June 2018

[viii] qz.com/1279371/this-physicists-ideas-of-time-will-blow-your-mind/

[ix] Healing the Heart of Democracy: The Courage to Create a Politics Worthy of the Human Spirit

[x] Healing the Heart of Democracy: The Courage to Create a Politics Worthy of the Human Spirit

[xi] www.goodreads.com/quotes/425033-it-matters-if-you-just-don-t-give-up

[xii] Frank Ostaseski, *The Five Invitations*, Bluebird Books for Life, 2017

Printed in Great Britain
by Amazon

22026236R00086